ELMHURST PUBLIC LIBRARY

3 1135 01992 3454

W9-AXK-828

J
531.6
Hei

ELMHURST PUBLIC LIBRARY
125 S. Prospect Avenue
Elmhurst, IL 60126-3298

WHAT IS MECHANICAL ENERGY?

KRISTINA LYN HEITKAMP

Britannica
Educational Publishing

IN ASSOCIATION WITH

ROSEN
EDUCATIONAL SERVICES

Published in 2018 by Britannica Educational Publishing (a trademark of Encyclopædia Britannica, Inc.) in association with The Rosen Publishing Group, Inc.
29 East 21st Street, New York, NY 10010

Copyright © 2018 The Rosen Publishing Group, Inc. and Encyclopædia Britannica, Inc. Encyclopædia Britannica, Britannica, and the Thistle logo are registered trademarks of Encyclopædia Britannica, Inc. All rights reserved.

Distributed exclusively by Rosen Publishing.
To see additional Britannica Educational Publishing titles, go to rosenpublishing.com.

First Edition

Britannica Educational Publishing
J.E. Luebering: Executive Director, Core Editorial
Mary Rose McCudden: Editor, Britannica Student Encyclopedia

Rosen Publishing
Amelie von Zumbusch: Editor
Nelson Sá: Art Director
Nicole Russo-Duca: Designer
Cindy Reiman: Photography Manager
Sherri Jackson: Photo Researcher

Library of Congress Cataloging-in-Publication Data

Names: Heitkamp, Kristina Lyn, author.
Title: What is mechanical energy? / Kristina Lyn Heitkamp.
Description: First edition. | New York, NY : Britannica Educational Publishing in association with Rosen Educational Services, 2018. | Series: Let's find out! Forms of energy | Includes bibliographical references and index. | Audience: 1–4.
Identifiers: LCCN 2016059470| ISBN 9781680487114 (library bound ; alk. paper) | ISBN 9781680487091 (pbk. ; alk. paper) | ISBN 9781680487107 (6-pack ; alk. paper)
Subjects: LCSH: Force and energy—Juvenile literature. | Power (Mechanics)—Juvenile literature.
Classification: LCC QC73.4 .H44 2018 | DDC 531/.6—dc23
LC record available at https://lccn.loc.gov/2016059470

Manufactured in the United States of America

Photo credits: Cover, p. 1 Billy Hustace/Iconica/Getty Images; p. 4 © iStockphoto.com/yenwen; p. 5 Sergey Novikov/Shutterstock.com; p. 6 arfabita/Shutterstock.com; p. 7 © Steve Lovegrove/Fotolia; pp. 8, 9, 12, 16 Encyclopædia Britannica, Inc.; p. 10 © Danny Warren/ Fotolia; p. 11 Aspen Photo/Shutterstock.com; p. 13 Anna Issakova/Shutterstock.com; p. 14 © iStockphoto.com/JerryGrugin; p. 15 PRNewsFoto/Silver Dollar City Attractions/AP Images; p. 17 khlungcenter/Shutterstock.com; p. 18 Monkey Business Images/Shutterstock.com; p 19 Pavel Losevsky/Hemera/Thinkstock, p. 20 stockvideoshooter/Shutterstock.com; p. 21 jgorzynik/SDhutterstock.com; p. 22 Samo Trebizan/Shutterstock.com; p. 23 © iStockphoto.com/Mimadeo; p. 24 © iStockphoto.com/SteveOehlenschlager, p. 25 airphoto. gr/Shutterstock.com; p. 26 elwynn/Shutterstock.com; p. 27 Ross Gordon Henry/Shutterstock.com; p. 28 Emma Farrer/Moment Open/ Getty Images; p. 29 Catalin Petolea/Shutterstock.com; interior pages background image Nevodka/Shutterstock.com.

Contents

What Is Energy?

Energy is another word for power, or the ability to do work. Energy makes things move. It makes machines work. Energy also makes living things grow. The sun is the source of almost all energy on Earth. The sun makes plants grow. When humans and animals eat the plants, they gain energy from the chemical energy that is stored in the plants. Humans get energy to move and run from eating food.

Energy exists in many different

Plants and people need energy. People get it from the food they eat, while plants get it from the sun.

Pushing pedals to make a bike move is a form of mechanical energy.

VOCABULARY

An **atom** is a tiny particle. Atoms are the building blocks of all matter.

forms. Electrical energy is used to power televisions and computers. This energy is created when particles called electrons move from one atom to another. Heat and light are also forms of energy. A dog's bark is an example of sound energy. The energy that an object or a body holds because of its motion and its position is called mechanical energy. Humans and machines use mechanical energy to do work.

POTENTIAL AND KINETIC ENERGY

Each of the different forms of energy can be described as either potential energy or kinetic energy. Potential energy is stored energy. For example, the chemical energy of food is stored energy. When people eat, their bodies change the stored energy into moving energy.

Potential energy can also come from the position of an object. For example, a rock on top of a hill has potential energy because it could roll down the hill.

Kinetic energy is moving energy.

This large rock is balanced on a hilltop. The rock has great potential energy.

Once the rock starts rolling down the hill it gains kinetic energy and loses potential energy. Electrical energy is kinetic energy because it consists of tiny particles called electrons that move from one atom to another.

These windsurfers are using the kinetic energy of wind to propel them forward.

THINK ABOUT IT

A player lifts a bowling ball, takes aim, and rolls it down the alley. The ball strikes all ten pins! Is this an example of potential or kinetic energy—or both?

MECHANICAL ENERGY

Mechanical energy is different from the other forms of energy because it can exist as both potential energy and kinetic energy. An object or a body possesses mechanical energy because of its motion (kinetic energy) and its position (potential energy).

An object can do work if it has mechanical energy. Machines use mechanical energy to perform work, such as cars driving on roads. Animals use mechanical energy to do work as

Mechanical energy can exist as both potential (stored) and kinetic (moving) energy.

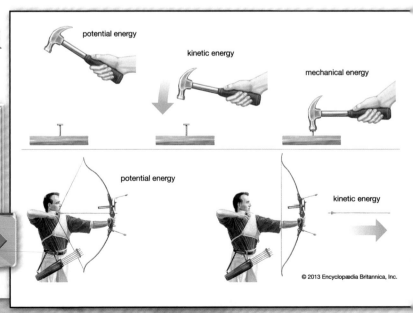

potential energy

kinetic energy

mechanical energy

potential energy

kinetic energy

© 2013 Encyclopædia Britannica, Inc.

Machines use mechanical energy—objects' stored and moving energy—to perform work.

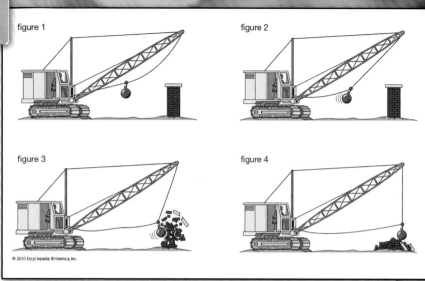

figure 1

figure 2

figure 3

figure 4

© 2010 Encyclopædia Britannica, Inc.

well, such as when birds fly through the air or fish swim in the sea.

Humans also use mechanical energy to do work. For instance, a person uses mechanical energy to score a goal in a soccer game. When the person's foot extends back, it has potential energy. When the foot kicks forward, the potential energy turns into kinetic energy to drive the ball into the goal.

THINK ABOUT IT

People use mechanical energy to swing back and forth on playground swings. At what point will the swing have the most potential energy?

POSITION AND MASS

Anything that takes up space is called matter. Air, water, rocks, and even people are examples of matter. Matter can be described by its mass. The mass of an object is the amount of material that makes up the object. The greater the mass of an object, the greater potential energy it can have. For instance, a bowling ball has more mass than a beach ball. The bowling ball at rest on a hill has more potential energy than the beach ball at rest on a hill.

Living things and nonliving things, such as a climber and a rock, are made up of matter.

A baseball player will hold a bat high to swing with great energy—which is needed to hit a home run.

THINK ABOUT IT

How can you tell that a bowling ball has more mass than a beach ball? What is inside each of them?

An object's height or position is another factor that determines its amount of potential energy. If an object has a great height or position, it will have greater energy than a similar object at a lower height.

CHANGING ENERGY

Energy cannot be created or destroyed. It can neither appear out of nowhere nor vanish into nowhere. One form of energy can be converted into another, though. Sometimes this happens naturally. For example, a person opening a door uses chemical energy stored in muscles. This energy is converted to mechanical energy of the moving muscle.

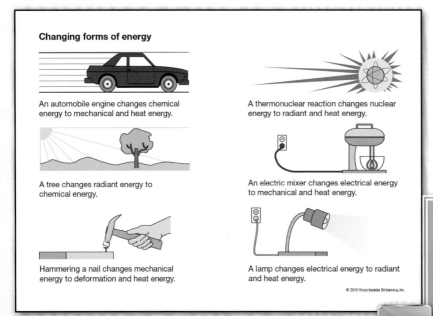

Changing forms of energy

An automobile engine changes chemical energy to mechanical and heat energy.

A thermonuclear reaction changes nuclear energy to radiant and heat energy.

A tree changes radiant energy to chemical energy.

An electric mixer changes electrical energy to mechanical and heat energy.

Hammering a nail changes mechanical energy to deformation and heat energy.

A lamp changes electrical energy to radiant and heat energy.

© 2010 Encyclopædia Britannica, Inc.

Energy can change from one form to another. It cannot be created or destroyed.

Chemical energy stored in the muscles converts to mechanical energy to do work, such as kicking a ball.

People have also learned how to use one form of energy to produce another. A battery is a device that stores power until it is needed. The stored power is in the form of chemical energy. That changes into electrical energy when the battery is used. In a light bulb, electrical energy changes to light and heat energy. A car's engine converts the chemical energy in fuel into moving mechanical energy.

COMPARE AND CONTRAST

How is the chemical energy that comes from food like the chemical energy that comes from car fuel? How is it different?

FINDING MECHANICAL ENERGY

Mechanical energy can be observed every day, even on the playground. Swinging on a swing set is an example of mechanical energy. Another example is playing on a slide. At the top of the slide, the body has the greatest potential energy and great height or position. The body has zero kinetic energy at this point because it is not moving. As

Swinging on a swing is just one of the ways to use mechanical energy on the playground.

14

As a rollercoaster climbs, its potential energy increases. As a rollercoaster falls, its kinetic energy increases.

VOCABULARY

Gravity is a force of attraction between objects that pulls objects together. The more mass an object has, the stronger its force of gravity, or pull, is. The planet Earth has more mass than anything on it so it pulls all things toward it.

the person slides down, the potential energy changes to kinetic energy. The total potential energy plus kinetic energy still equals the same amount of mechanical energy. In this case, the force of gravity helps provide the kinetic energy.

DOING WORK

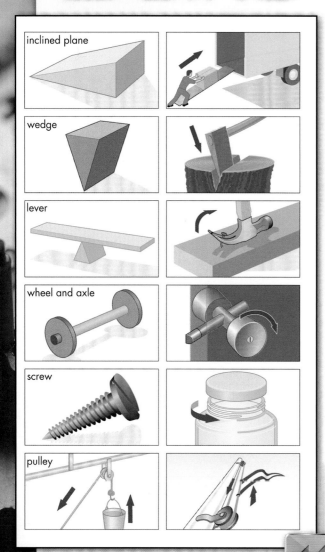

inclined plane

wedge

lever

wheel and axle

screw

pulley

Machines—from simple tools such as wedges, levers, and pulleys to complex devices such as automobiles—use mechanical energy to do work. A demolition machine is a good example. The machine's huge wrecking ball has great mass. As the ball swings backward, its high position holds great potential energy. When the ball swings forward and hits

Simple machines use mechanical energy to do work.

a structure, the force or work of mechanical energy brings down the structure.

Humans also use the mechanical energy of simple tools to do work. For instance, a hammer has mechanical energy when it is used to drive a nail into a board. When the hammer is raised, it has potential energy from the work done in lifting it. When the hammer is moved toward the nail, the potential energy becomes kinetic energy, which can do the work of driving the nail into the board.

THINK ABOUT IT

There are many examples of mechanical energy in nature, too. What work gets done from the mechanical energy of a river?

The hammer's potential energy and kinetic energy do the work of nailing a board.

EVERYDAY ENERGY

There are many ways that we use mechanical energy in our daily lives. All actions done by the body, such as lifting a fork to the mouth, require mechanical energy. Human bodies convert the chemical energy found in food into energy to fuel movements. Even when the body is at rest, the human heart constantly transforms the body's

People get chemical energy from the foods that they eat every day.

Motorcycle engines convert chemical energy in fuel into mechanical energy that makes the wheels move.

stored fuel into the mechanical energy of blood pumping throughout the body.

Sometimes our actions themselves lead to other uses of mechanical energy. Flipping on a fan's switch converts the electrical energy into mechanical energy that makes the fan's blades turn and move.

THINK ABOUT IT

Inventors have built dance floors that convert mechanical energy produced by dancing feet into electrical energy to power lights and more! Can you think of other ways that mechanical energy can be converted to another form of energy?

HISTORY OF MECHANICAL ENERGY

People have used mechanical energy to do work for thousands of years. Waterpower was used to grind grain during the Middle Ages. Later, people used the mechanical energy of wind to do work. Windmills were used to grind grain into flour and to pump water. Today modern windmills, called wind turbines, produce electricity for many communities.

Early water mills used the mechanical energy of moving water to do work.

VOCABULARY

Turbines are engines that depend on moving water, steam, or air to spin a series of blades.

The Industrial Revolution was a period of major changes in the way products were made. More than 200 years ago people began to invent machines to do the work that individuals did by hand before that time. People also built factories where those machines could be used to make many products at once. Inventors created power sources to run the machines. For example, steam engines used the power of steam to produce mechanical energy. They were used for many years to power trains, cars, ships, and other machines.

Steam engines in trains convert heat energy into mechanical energy.

RENEWABLE ENERGY

The sources of energy used to power the simplest machines are renewable, which means that they are not likely to run out. Examples include the sun, wind, and water. Water and wind were used to operate mills for hundreds of years because there was a constant supply of both.

Hydroelectric plants generate electricity from the kinetic energy of moving water.

Wind farms can be found all over the world. They work best in wide open, windy areas.

Today, machines are more complicated. They rely on other sources of power, such as electricity. However, the renewable energy sources are still useful. When the blades of a wind turbine spin, they convert mechanical energy of the wind into electrical energy. Wind turbines can work alone or in a group, called a wind farm. In a similar way, other machines in rivers and oceans can use the mechanical energy of moving water to produce electrical energy. That electrical energy can then be used to power large machines.

THINK ABOUT IT

Certain places have better renewable energy sources than others. What renewable energy sources exist where you live?

NONRENEWABLE ENERGY

All the machines of modern life use mechanical energy to do work, but these machines often need another form of energy to make them run. Wind and water power are used to create some of that energy. However, about ninety percent of the energy comes from burning fossil fuels. Fossil fuels include petroleum (oil),

Oil wells pump up petroleum from deep inside Earth and store it at the surface.

coal, and natural gas. The burning of these fossil fuels produces heat. The heat energy is often converted into mechanical or electrical energy.

THINK ABOUT IT

Why can't we replace fossil fuels once they are used? How long does it take for them to form?

Fossil fuels, like fossils, are the remains of plants and animals that lived long ago. These resources can take thousands or millions of years to form. The planet's supply of fossil fuels is limited. Fossil fuels are called nonrenewable resources. Once they are used up, they will be gone forever.

A fossil fuel power plant burns oil, coal, or natural gas to produce electricity.

PROBLEMS WITH ENERGY

For hundreds of years people and industries have relied on fossil fuels to generate energy.

However, fossil fuels are nonrenewable. They also harm the environment. When petroleum and coal burn, they release harmful gases. These cause pollution, which can make people sick or make it hard for people to breathe. Scientists think that burning fossil fuels also add extra gases to the air that trap heat in the atmosphere. They think that this

Burning fossil fuels, such as gasoline, can cause air pollution.

Droughts can reduce the amount of running water available to produce hydroelectic power.

has led to a problem called global warming. Many people want to use renewable energy sources instead of fossil fuels. Renewable energy sources such as wind, water, and solar power will not run out. However, switching to these energy sources is expensive. People would have to make major changes to the systems that are already in place. In addition, some technologies for renewable energy are still relatively new. They need further research and development.

COMPARE AND CONTRAST

What are some advantages and disadvantages to using alternative energy sources and fossil fuels?

Reducing Energy Use

Conservation is the protection of things found in nature. People who care about conservation try to preserve natural resources so they will still be around in the future. They also try to keep the environment clean and healthy.

Conservation can be hard because it can require people to give up some conveniences. For example, cars that run on

You conserve energy when you turn off the lights as you leave a room.

People who choose to ride less in a car and walk more get more exercise.

THINK ABOUT IT

Conserving nonrenewable energy sources can involve healthful, fun exercise! What sports activities that involve the use of mechanical energy by your body do you most enjoy doing?

gasoline are everywhere. They make traveling easy, but they also produce a lot of air pollution. To have cleaner air, people can choose to drive less and walk more. Understanding where our energy comes from is a responsibility we have. We can choose to use the mechanical energy from our legs to walk rather than to use nonrenewable energy sources by riding in cars.

GLOSSARY

alternative Offering or expressing a choice.

atmosphere The layer of gases that surrounds Earth.

battery A container that stores chemical energy and converts it to electric energy when used.

chemical energy The energy that is stored in the bonds that hold the particles of matter together.

conservation Protecting all things found in nature.

electron An elementary particle that has a negative charge of electricity and travels around the nucleus, or center, of an atom.

environment The physical surroundings on Earth, such as air, oceans, and trees.

global warming A steady rise in the average temperature of Earth's surface.

Industrial Revolution A period in history beginning in the 1700s when people began to use machines to make products.

lever A bar used to pry or move something.

Middle Ages A period in European history that came between ancient and modern times and lasted from about 500 to 1500 CE.

natural resources Something found in nature that can be used by people, such as sunlight, water, or plants.

pollution Contamination by waste, chemicals, or other harmful substances.

pulley A small wheel with a rope or chain around its edge, used to change the direction of the force applied for lifting.

wedge A piece of wood or metal with a pointed edge used especially to split wood or rocks and to lift heavy weights.

For More Information

Books

Berne, Emma Carlson. *Speeding!: Mechanical Energy*. New York, NY: Rosen Publishing, 2013.

Bright, Michael. *From Sunshine to Light Bulb: Source to Resource*. New York, NY: Crabtree Publishing Company, 2016.

Claybourne, Anna. *Experiments with Energy: First Science Experiments*. New York, NY: Rosen Publishing, 2017.

Einspruch, Andrew. *What Is Energy? Discovery Education: How It Works*. New York, NY: Rosen Publishing, 2013.

Kamkwamba, William. *The Boy Who Harnessed the Wind* (Young Readers Edition). New York, NY: Penguin, 2015.

Sneideman, Joshua and Erin Twamley. *Renewable Energy: Discover the Fuel of the Future With 20 Projects*. White River Junction, VT: Nomad Press, 2016.

Websites

Because of the changing nature of internet links, Rosen Publishing has developed an online list of websites related to the subject of this book. This site is updated regularly. Please use this link to access the list:

http://www.rosenlinks.com/LFO/mechanical

INDEX